Anne of
Green
Gables

빨간 머리 앤

두근두근 확장 영어 01

Anne of Green Gables 빨간 머리 앤

© 선진호 2020

초판 1쇄 인쇄 2020년 8월 27일
초판 1쇄 발행 2020년 9월 17일

원작 루시 모드 몽고메리 | **편저** 선진호
펴낸이 박지혜

기획·편집 박지혜 | **마케팅** 윤해승 최향모
디자인 this-cover | **일러스트레이션** this-cover
제작 더블비

펴낸곳 ㈜멀리깊이
출판등록 2020년 6월 1일 제406-2020-000057호
주소 10881 경기도 파주시 광인사길 127
전자우편 murly@munhak.com
편집 070-4234-3241 | **마케팅** 02-2039-9463 | **팩스** 02-2039-9460
인스타그램 @murly_books
페이스북 @murlybooks

ISBN 979-11-971396-1-1 14740
     979-11-971396-0-4 (세트)

두근두근
확장 영어 01

빨간 머리 앤

책장만 넘기면 문장이 완성되는 완벽한 어순 학습법

Anne

of

Green

Gables

원작 루시 모드 몽고메리 **편저** 선진호

멀린키즈

"난 영어를 못해."

아마도 대한민국의 많은 영어 학습자들이 이런 생각을 하겠지만 의외로 여러분은 많은 양의 영단어를 알고 있습니다. 책상, 자동차, 나무, 하늘 등 눈앞에 보이는 대부분의 영어 이름을 알고 있을 정도니까요. 그럼에도 불구하고 영어가 어려운 이유는 뭘까요? 아마도 어순 때문이겠지요.

영어의 어순은 한국어와 정반대입니다. 이미 우리 머릿속에서 공고하게 완성된 어순 체계를 모두 해체해서 내뱉으려니 머릿속은 뒤죽박죽이 되어버리지요. 그러니 차근차근 영어 어순을 학습하는 과정이 반드시 필요합니다. 차근차근 한 단어씩 순서대로 늘려 나갈 수만 있다면 긴 문장을 말하는 일도 어려운 일이 아니게 됩니다.

두근두근 확장 영어 시리즈는 바로 이 어순을 완벽하게 학습할 수 있도록 구성했습니다. 책장을 넘기다 보면 어느새 긴 문장이 완성되어 있게끔요. 더욱 즐겁게 학습하실 수 있도록 한국인이 사랑하는 명작을 확장형 어순 프로그램에 맞춰 구성했습니다. 아마도 이 책을 모두 학습하고 나면, 원서 한 권을 읽은 듯한 감동과 뿌듯함을 느끼실 수 있을 거예요.

모든 확장형 문장이 듣고 빈칸을 채우는 딕테이션(dictation)으로 구성되었다는 것도 큰 장점입니다. 딕테이션만큼 몰입해서 학습하기에 좋은 방법이 없지요. 패턴이 길어지는 과정을 반복적으로 듣고 적는 훈련을 통해 자연스럽게 어순을 익힐 수 있을 겁니다.

여러분이 원서 속의 주인공들을 만날 생각을 하니 무척이나 설렙니다. 이 책이 여러분의 사랑을 듬뿍 받을 수 있도록 손을 모아봅니다.

2020년 선진호

책장만 넘기세요.
문장이 저절로 길어집니다!

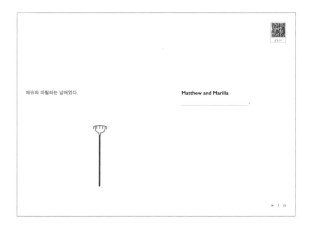

❶ 모든 문장은 영어에서 가장 많이 쓰는 기본 패턴으로 구성했습니다. 책장을 넘길 때마다 영어의 어순대로 문장이 늘어나기 때문에, 우리말과 다른 영어 어순을 자연스럽게 익힐 수 있습니다.

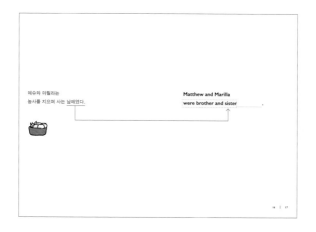

매슈와 마릴라는
농사를 지으며 사는 남매였다.

Matthew and Marilla
were brother and sister.

❷ 책장을 넘기면 앞 페이지에 있던 빈칸 문장이 자연스럽게 완성됩니다. 모르는 표현이 나와도 당황하지 마세요. 책장을 넘기면, 정답이 보입니다!

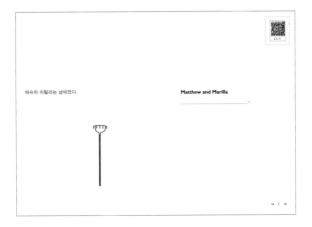

배슈와 마릴라는 남매였다.

Matthew and Marilla

14 | 15

* 확장형 문장이 시작하는 모든 페이지에는 듣기용 QR코드가 있습니다. 자
  연스럽게 빈칸을 채우는 딕테이션(dictation: 들리는 대로 받아쓰기) 학습을 할
  수 있어, 최상의 집중력으로 단기간에 어학 실력을 끌어올릴 수 있습니다.
* 스마트폰 카메라로 QR코드를 찍으시면 듣기 파일이 재생됩니다.
* https://cafe.naver.com/murlybooks 에 들어오시면 mp3 파일을 다
  운로드 받으실 수 있습니다.

줄거리 문장을 읽으세요.
자연스럽게 원서 전체를 읽게 됩니다.

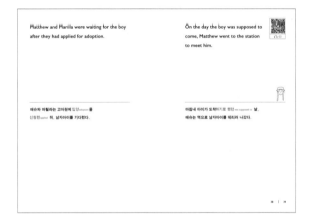

Matthew and Marilla were waiting for the boy after they had applied for adoption.

On the day the boy was supposed to come, Matthew went to the station to meet him.

매슈와 마릴라는 고아원에 입양apply for 을 신청한apply for 뒤, 남자아이를 기다렸다.

마침내 아이가 도착하기로 했던was supposed to 날, 매슈는 역으로 남자아이를 데리러 나갔다.

* 확장형 문장으로 패턴을 익힌다면, 줄거리 문장을 통해 원서 읽기의 기쁨을 느낄 수 있습니다. 모두가 알지만 누구도 읽어 본 적 없는 원서 읽기! 두근두근 확장 시리즈로 경험해 보세요!

전문을 읽으세요.
두 배로 오래 기억하게 됩니다.

Matthew and Marilla were brother and sister farming in Avonlea in Edward Island in Canada. They wanted to adopt a boy to help them to farm because neither of them had married even though they were middle age. Matthew and Marilla were waiting for the boy after they had applied for adoption. On the day the boy was supposed to come, Matthew went to the station to meet him. But, it was a skinny girl with red hair and freckles in her face that the orphanage sent them.

"Matthew, who's she! Where is the boy?"

"There wasn't any boy," said Matthew.

"There was only HER."

He nodded at the child remembering that he had never even asked her name.

"No boy! But we sent word to the orphanage to bring a boy."

"I couldn't leave her at the station alone no matter where the mistake

During this dialogue, the child was silent looking from one to the other.

Suddenly, she dropped her precious bag and sprang forward a step clasping her hands and yelled out.

"You don't want me because I'm not a boy? Nobody ever wanted me. I forgot that nobody had ever wanted me."

Matthew persuaded Marilla.

"Well, she's a real nice little thing, Marilla. It's kind of a pity to send her back when she wants to stay here so much. Think about it. She could be your good friend to talk to."

Matthew thought of Anne who was happy calling the ordinary path lined with apple trees a white road of joy, on his way home. Matthew kind of liked the talkative little girl. Matthew decided not to send her back. And that is how Anne began to live in the house with the green gables. Matthew and Marilla lived happily because of talkative Anne who was a child of imagination. Anne started a joyful journey with her best friend, Diana at school.

One September morning, Anne and Diana, two of the happiest little girls in Avonlea, were walking on the street to the school blithely.

"I guess Gilbert Blythe will be in school today," said Diana.

"He's been visiting his cousins. He's awfully handsome, Anne. And he teases the girls so much. He just torments them."

But, Diana's voice indicated that she rather liked having her life tormented than not.

* 확장형 문장과 줄거리 문장으로 익힌 필수 영어 패턴을 한 번에 정리할 수 있습니다. 출퇴근길이나 잠들기 전, 듣기 파일을 들으며 전체 문장을 소리 내어 읽어 보세요. 긴 문장 말하기, 여러분도 해낼 수 있습니다!

Contents

Anne of Green Gables

매슈와 마릴라는 남매였다.

🎧 01

Matthew and Marilla

매슈와 마릴라는
농사를 지으며 사는 **남매였다.**

Matthew and Marilla
were brother and sister_____.

매슈와 마릴라는

에이번리 마을에서

농사를 지으며 사는 남매였다.

Matthew and Marilla

were brother and sister farming

_____ .

* Avonlea 에이번리 (마을)

매슈와 마릴라는 에드워드 섬
에이번리 마을에서
농사를 지으며 사는 남매였다.

Matthew and Marilla
were brother and sister farming
in Avonlea _____.

매슈와 마릴라는 캐나다의
에드워드 섬 에이번리 마을에서
농사를 지으며 사는 남매였다.

Matthew and Marilla

were brother and sister farming

in Avonlea in Edward Island _____ .

매슈와 마릴라는 캐나다의
에드워드 섬 에이번리 마을에서
농사를 지으며 사는 남매였다.

Matthew and Marilla

were brother and sister farming

in Avonlea in Edward Island in Canada.

그들은 남자아이 하나를 입양하길 **원했다.**

They wanted _____.

* **adopt** 입양하다

그들은 그들을 도와줄
남자아이 하나를 입양하길 원했다.

They wanted to adopt a boy

_____.

그들은 농사일을 도와줄 남자아이 하나를
입양하길 원했다.

They wanted to adopt a boy

to help them _____ .

둘 중 누구도 결혼하지 않았기 때문에
그들은 농사일을 도와줄
남자아이 하나를 입양하길 원했다.

They wanted to adopt a boy

to help them to farm _____

_____ .

중년의 나이에도 불구하고 **둘 중 누구도**
결혼하지 않았기 때문에
그들은 농사일을 도와줄
남자아이 하나를 입양하길 원했다.

They wanted to adopt a boy

to help them to farm because neither of them

had married

_____ .

* even though ~에도 불구하고
* middle age 중년

중년의 나이에도 불구하고 둘 중 누구도
결혼하지 않았기 때문에
그들은 농사일을 도와줄
남자아이 하나를 입양하길 원했다.

They wanted to adopt a boy
to help them to farm because neither of them
had married
even though they were middle age.

Matthew and Marilla were waiting for the boy after they had applied for adoption.

매슈와 마릴라는 고아원에 입양_{adoption}을 신청한_{applied} 뒤, 남자아이를 기다렸다.

On the day the boy was supposed to come, Matthew went to the station to meet him.

마침내 아이가 도착하기로 했던_{was supposed to} 날,
매슈는 역으로 남자아이를 데리러 나갔다.

하지만 그 아이는 삐쩍 마른 여자아이였다.

But, it was _____.

* skinny 삐쩍 마른, 깡마른

하지만 그 아이는

빨간 머리에 삐쩍 마른 여자아이였다.

But, it was a skinny girl

_____.

하지만 그 아이는
주근깨투성이인 얼굴에 빨간 머리를 한
삐쩍 마른 여자아이였다.

But, it was a skinny girl
with red hair

_____ .

* freckle 주근깨

하지만 고아원에서 그들에게 보내온 아이는
주근깨투성이인 얼굴에 빨간 머리를 한
삐쩍 마른 여자아이였다.

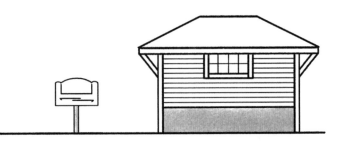

But, it was a skinny girl

with red hair and freckles in her face

_____ .

* orphanage 고아원

하지만 고아원에서 그들에게 보내온 아이는
주근깨투성이인 얼굴에 빨간 머리를 한
삐쩍 마른 여자아이였다.

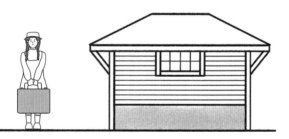

But, it was a skinny girl
with red hair and freckles in her face
that the orphanage sent to them.

"Matthew, who's she? Where is the boy?"

"There wasn't any boy," said Matthew.

"There was only HER."

"매슈 오라버니! 저 아인 누구죠?
  남자아인 어디 있나요?"
"남자아인 없었어. 저 아이뿐이었다고."
매슈가 말했다.

He nodded at the child
remembering that he had never even
asked her name.

"No boy! But we sent word to orphanage
to bring a boy."

그는 아이의 이름도 물어보지 않았다는
사실을 떠올리며 고갯짓으로 아이를 가리켰다.

"맙소사! 하지만 우리는 고아원에 남자아이를 데려다 달라고
 부탁했어요."

"이 아이를 두고 올 수는 없었어."

"I couldn't _____ her."

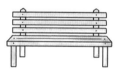

"이 아이를 그 역에 두고 올 수는 없었어."

"I couldn't leave her _____."

"이 아이를 그 역에 혼자 두고 올 수는 없었어."

"I couldn't leave her at the station _____."

"뭐가 어디서 잘못된 건진 몰라도

이 아이를 그 역에 혼자 두고 올 수는 없었어."

"I couldn't leave her at the station alone

_____

_____."

"뭐가 어디서 잘못된 건진 몰라도

 이 아이를 그 역에 혼자 두고 올 수는 없었어."

"I couldn't leave her at the station alone
no matter where the mistake had come in."

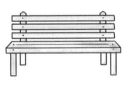

이런 이야기가 오가는 동안,

_____ **this dialogue,**

* **during** (특정 기간) 동안, ~하는 사이에

이런 이야기가 오가는 동안,

아이는 잠자코 있었다.

During this dialogue,

_____ .

* silent 조용한, 고요한

이런 이야기가 오가는 동안,
아이는 두 사람을 번갈아 바라보며
잠자코 있었다.

During this dialogue,

the child was silent

_____.

이런 이야기가 오가는 동안,
아이는 두 사람을 번갈아 바라보며
잠자코 있었다.

During this dialogue,

the child was silent

looking from one to the other.

Suddenly, she dropped her precious bag and
sprang forward a step clasping her hands and
yelled out.

갑자기|suddenly 아이가 그녀의 소중한precious 가방을 툭
떨어뜨리더니dropped 두 손을 꼭 쥔 채clasping her hands 한 발짝
앞으로 나와 소리쳤다yelled out.

"You don't want me because I'm not
a boy! Nobody ever wanted me."

🎧 08

"제가 남자아이가 아니라서 필요 없으신 거죠!
 아무도 저를 원한 적이 없어요."

"난 그걸 잊고 있었어요."

"I forgot _____.

"난 아무도 절 원하지 않았다는 걸
잊고 있었어요."

"I forgot that

_____."

"난 아무도 절 원한 적이 없다는 걸
잊고 있었어요."

"I forgot that

nobody _____ wanted me."

"난 아무도 절 원한 적이 없다는 걸
잊고 있었어요."

"I forgot that

nobody had ever wanted me."

Matthew persuaded Marilla.

"Well, she's a real nice little thing, Marilla.

매슈는 마릴라를 설득했다persuaded.

"글쎄다, 저 앤 정말로 좋은 아이야, 마릴라.

It's kind of a pity to send her back when she wants to stay here so much. Think about it. She could be your good friend to talk to."

그렇게 여기 있고 싶어 하는데 다시 돌려보낸다는 게 너무 안됐잖아. 생각해 봐. 저 애가 너의 좋은 이야기 상대가 될 수도 있어."

매슈는 앤을 떠올렸다.

Matthew thought _____ .

매슈는 행복해하는 앤을 떠올렸다.

Matthew thought of Anne _____.

매슈는 평범한 길을 부르며
행복해하던 앤을 떠올렸다.

Matthew thought of Anne who was happy

_____ .

* ordinary 평범한
* path 좁은 길

매슈는 사과나무들이 늘어선
평범한 길을 부르며
행복해하던 앤을 떠올렸다.

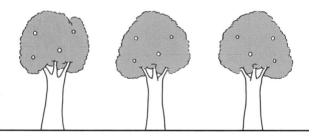

Matthew thought of Anne who was happy
calling the ordinary path

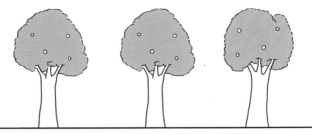

매슈는 사과나무들이 늘어선

평범한 길을

하얀 길이라 부르며 행복해하던 앤을 떠올렸다.

Matthew thought of Anne who was happy

calling the ordinary path

lined with apple trees

_____ .

매슈는 사과나무들이 늘어선
평범한 길을 기쁨의
하얀 길이라 부르며
행복해하던 앤을 떠올렸다.

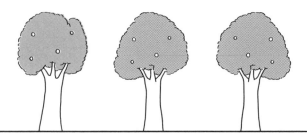

Matthew thought of Anne who was happy

calling the ordinary path

lined with apple trees a white road

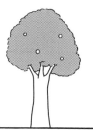

매슈는 집으로 오는 길에
사과나무들이 늘어선
평범한 길을 기쁨의 하얀 길이라 부르며
행복해하던 앤을 떠올렸다.

Matthew thought of Anne who was happy

calling the ordinary path

lined with apple trees a white road

of joy _____

매슈는 집으로 오는 길에
사과나무들이 늘어선
평범한 길을 기쁨의 하얀 길이라 부르며
행복해하던 앤을 떠올렸다.

Matthew thought of Anne who was happy
calling the ordinary path
lined with apple trees a white road
of joy on his way home.

Matthew kind of liked the talkative little girl.
Marilla decided not to send her back. And
that is how Anne began to live in the house
with the green gables.

매슈는 수다쟁이 작은 소녀가 싫지 않았다. 마릴라는 앤을 돌려
보내지 않기로 결심했다. 이렇게 해서 앤은 초록지붕 집에서 살
게 되었다.

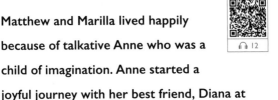

Matthew and Marilla lived happily
because of talkative Anne who was a
child of imagination. Anne started a
joyful journey with her best friend, Diana at
school.

매슈와 마릴라는 수다스럽고talkative 상상력imagination이 풍부한
앤 덕분에 행복하게 생활할 수 있었다. 앤은 단짝 친구 다이애
나를 만나 즐거운 학교생활을 했다.

9월의 어느 날 아침,

앤과 다이애나는 걷고 있었다.

One September morning,

9월의 어느 날 아침, 가장 행복한 두 명의
작은 소녀들인 앤과 다이애나는 걷고 있었다.

One September morning,

Anne and Diana,

_____ were walking.

9월의 어느 날 아침, 에이번리 마을에서
가장 행복한 두 명의 작은 소녀들인
앤과 다이애나는 걷고 있었다.

One September morning,

Anne and Diana,

two of the happiest little girls _____,

were walking.

9월의 어느 날 아침, 에이번리 마을에서
가장 행복한 두 명의 작은 소녀들인
앤과 다이애나는 길을 걷고 있었다.

One September morning,

Anne and Diana,

two of the happiest little girls in Avonlea,

were walking _____.

9월의 어느 날 아침, 에이번리 마을에서
가장 행복한 두 명의 작은 소녀들인
앤과 다이애나는 학교로 향하는 길을 걷고 있었다.

One September morning,

Anne and Diana,

two of the happiest little girls in Avonlea,

were walking on the street

_____.

9월의 어느 날 아침, 에이번리 마을에서
가장 행복한 두 명의 작은 소녀들인
앤과 다이애나는 즐겁게 학교로 향하는 길을 걷고 있
었다.

One September morning,

Anne and Diana,

two of the happiest little girls in Avonlea,

were walking on the street

to the school _____.

* blithely 즐겁게, 쾌활하게

9월의 어느 날 아침, 에이번리 마을에서
가장 행복한 두 명의 작은 소녀들인
앤과 다이애나는 즐겁게 학교로 향하는 길을 걷고 있
었다.

One September morning,
Anne and Diana,
two of the happiest little girls in Avonlea,
were walking on the street
to the school blithely.

"I guess Gilbert Blythe will be in school

today," said Diana.

"He's been visiting his cousins.

He's awfully handsome, Anne.

다이애나가 말했다.

"길버트 블라이스가 오늘 학교에 올 것 같아.

 사촌 집에 가 있었대. 대단히awfully 잘생긴 친구야, 앤.

And he teases the girls so much.

He just torments them."

그리고 여자애들을 괴롭히길 좋아해.

그 애는 아예 우리 일상을 헤집어놓는다니깐torment."

하지만 다이애나의 목소리는 드러내고 있었다.

But, Diana's voice _____.

* **indicated** 은연 중에 나타냈다(원 indicate)

하지만 다이애나의 목소리는 그녀가
차라리 더 좋아하고 있음을 **드러내고 있었다.**

But, Diana's voice indicated

_____ .

* **rather** 오히려, 차라리

하지만 다이애나의 목소리는
그녀가 그녀의 일상을 갖는 편을
차라리 더 좋아하고 있음을 드러내고 있었다.

But, Diana's voice indicated

that she rather liked _____ .

하지만 다이애나의 목소리는
그녀가 그녀의 일상이 헤집어지는 편을
차라리 더 좋아하고 있음을 드러내고 있었다.

But, Diana's voice indicated
that she rather liked having her life

_____ .

* **tormented** 헤집어지는 (원 torment)

하지만 다이애나의 목소리는
그녀가 그녀의 일상이 헤집어지는 편을
그렇지 않은 것보다 차라리 더 좋아하고 있음을
드러내고 있었다.

But, Diana's voice indicated
that she rather liked having her life
tormented _____.

하지만 다이애나의 목소리는
그녀가 그녀의 일상이 헤집어지는 편을
그렇지 않은 것보다 차라리 더 좋아하고 있음을
드러내고 있었다.

But, Diana's voice indicated
that she rather liked having her life
tormented than not.

"You'll have Gilbert in your class after this,"
said Diana.

"길버트는 너랑 같은 반에 들어갈 거야.
다이애나가 말했다.

"And he used to be the head of his
class, I can tell you. You won't find
it so easy to be first place after this,
Anne."

그 앤 반에서 1등을 도맡아 하곤 했어.
이제 네가 계속 1등 하기가 쉽지 않을 거야, 앤."

필립스 선생님이 교실
뒤에 있을 때,

When Mr. Phillips was _____

of the classroom,

**필립스 선생님이 교실 뒤에서
라틴어를 듣고 있을 때,**

When Mr. Phillips was in the back

of the classroom _____,

* **Latin** 라틴어, 라틴계 사람

필립스 선생님이 교실 뒤에서

학생 중 하나의

라틴어를 듣고 있을 때,

When Mr. Phillips was in the back
of the classroom hearing Latin

_____ ,

필립스 선생님이 교실 뒤에서
학생 중 하나의
라틴어를 듣고 있을 때,
다이애나가 속삭였다.

When Mr. Phillips was in the back
of the classroom hearing Latin
from one of the students,

_____.

필립스 선생님이 교실 뒤에서
학생 중 하나의
라틴어를 듣고 있을 때,
다이애나가 앤에게 속삭였다.

When Mr. Phillips was in the back
of the classroom hearing Latin
from one of the students,
Diana whispered _____.

필립스 선생님이 교실 뒤에서
학생 중 하나의
라틴어를 듣고 있을 때,
다이애나가 앤에게 속삭였다.

When Mr. Phillips was in the back
of the classroom hearing Latin
from one of the students,
Diana whispered to Anne.

"쟤가 **길버트 블라이스**야."

🎧 18

"_____ Gilbert Blythe."

"바로 저기에 앉아 있는 **애가 길버트 블라이스야.**"

"That's Gilbert Blythe _____."

"통로를 사이에 두고 건너편에

앉아 있는 애가 길버트 블라이스야."

"That's Gilbert Blythe sitting right

_____ ."

* aisle 통로

"통로를 사이에 두고 네 건너편에
앉아 있는 애가 길버트 블라이스야, 앤."

"That's Gilbert Blythe sitting right across the aisle _____, Anne."

"통로를 사이에 두고 네 건너편에

　앉아 있는 애가 길버트 블라이스야, 앤."

"That's Gilbert Blythe sitting right across the aisle from you, Anne."

"그를 한 번 봐."

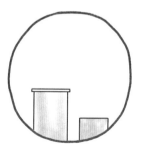

"Just _____ him."

"네가 그렇게 생각하지 않는지 어떤지
　그를 한 번 봐."

"Just look at him

_____."

" 잘생겼는지

  어떤지 그를 한 번 봐."

"Just look at him

   and see if you don't think

_____."

"잘생겼는지 어떤지 그를 한 번 봐."

"Just look at him
and see if you don't think he's handsome."

앤에게는 그렇게 할 좋은 기회가 있었다.

She _____ **to do so.**

길버트 블라이스는 마침 정신이 없었기 때문에
앤은 그렇게 할 좋은 기회가 있었다.

She had a good chance to do so

_____ .

길버트 블라이스는 마침
한 여자아이의 길게 땋은 금발을
핀으로 고정시켜 주느라 **정신이 없었기 때문에**
앤은 그렇게 할 좋은 기회가 있었다.

She had a good chance to do so
because Gilbert Blythe was busy

_____.

* pinning 핀 고정하기
* braid 땋은 머리

길버트 블라이스는 마침
앞자리에 앉은 한 여자아이의 길게 땋은 금발을
핀으로 고정시켜 주느라 정신이 없었기 때문에
앤은 그렇게 할 좋은 기회가 있었다.

She had a good chance to do so
because Gilbert Blythe was busy
pinning the long yellow braid of a girl

_____ .

* in front of ~의 앞에, 정면에

길버트 블라이스는 마침
앞자리에 앉은 한 여자아이의 길게 땋은 금발을
의자 등받이에 핀으로
고정시켜 주느라 정신이 없었기 때문에
앤은 그렇게 할 좋은 기회가 있었다.

She had a good chance to do so
because Gilbert Blythe was busy
pinning the long yellow braid of a girl
who sat in front of him

길버트 블라이스는 마침
앞자리에 앉은 한 여자아이의 길게 땋은 금발을
의자 등받이에 핀으로
고정시켜 주느라 정신이 없었기 때문에
앤은 그렇게 할 좋은 기회가 있었다.

She had a good chance to do so
because Gilbert Blythe was busy
pinning the long yellow braid of a girl
who sat in front of him
to the back of her seat.

이윽고 루비 길리스가 일어섰다.

🎧 21

Presently Ruby Gillis _____.

이윽고 루비 길리스가

선생님께 수학 문제 답을 이야기하려고 **일어섰다.**

Presently Ruby Gillis stood up

_____ .

이윽고 루비 길리스가 선생님께 수학 문제 답을
이야기하려고 일어서는 순간,
그녀는 의자에 도로 주저앉았다.

Presently Ruby Gillis stood up
to give the math answer to the teacher;

_____.

이윽고 루비 길리스가 선생님께 수학 문제 답을
이야기하려고 일어서는 순간,
그녀는 비명을 지르며 의자에 도로 주저앉았다.

Presently Ruby Gillis stood up
to give the math answer to the teacher;
she fell back into her seat _____
_____.

* shriek (날카로운) 비명

이윽고 루비 길리스가 선생님께 수학 문제 답을
이야기하려고 일어서는 순간,
그녀는 머리카락이 통째로 빠지는 듯한 고통에
비명을 지르며 의자에 도로 주저앉았다.

Presently Ruby Gillis stood up
to give the math answer to the teacher;
she fell back into her seat with a little shriek,

_____

_____.

* **pulled** 당겨졌다(원 pull)
* **roots** (머리카락, 손톱, 치아 등의) 뿌리(부분)들

이윽고 루비 길리스가 선생님께 수학 문제 답을
이야기하려고 일어서는 순간,
그녀는 머리카락이 통째로 빠지는 듯한 고통에
비명을 지르며 의자에 도로 주저앉았다.

Presently Ruby Gillis stood up
to give the math answer to the teacher;
she fell back into her seat with a little shriek,
believing that her hair was pulled out by the
roots.

She began to cry and Gilbert had whisked the pin out of sight and was studying his history with the soberest face in the world. But after this, he looked at Anne and winked.

그녀가 울기 시작하자, 길버트는 보이지 않게 얼른 핀을 치우고는had whisked 세상에서 가장 진지한the soberest 얼굴로 역사 공부를 하는 척했다. 하지만 소란이 가라앉자 앤을 바라보며 익살스런 몸짓으로 한쪽 눈을 찡긋해winked 보였다.

After school, Anne confided to Diana
"I think your Gilbert Blythe is
handsome. But I think he's very
bold."

학교가 끝나자, 앤이 다이애나에게 솔직히 말했다confided.
"네가 말한 길버트 블라이스는 잘생기긴 했어.
하지만 아주 뻔뻔한bold 것 같아."

"더군다나, 그건 예의 없는 짓이야."

"Moreover, it _____."

"더군다나, 윙크를 하는 건 예의 없는 짓이야."

"Moreover, it isn't good manners _____."

“더군다나, 처음 보는 여자에게

　윙크를 하는 건 예의 없는 짓이야.”

"Moreover, it isn't good manners to wink

_____."

* strange 낯선, 미지의

"더군다나, 처음 보는 여자에게
　윙크를 하는 건 예의 없는 짓이야."

"Moreover, it isn't good manners to wink at a strange girl."

Gilbert Blythe was trying to make Anne Shirley look at him and failing utterly,
because Anne was at that moment totally
oblivious not only to the very existence of
Gilbert Blythe, but of every other student in
Avonlea school itself.

길버트 블라이스는 앤 셜리의 시선을 끌려고 애썼지만 완전히
utterly 실패였다.
앤은 그 순간moment 길버트뿐만 아니라 에이번리 학교 학생
모두와 학교 그 자체를 깡그리 잊고 있었다totally oblivious.

With her chin propped on her hands and her eyes fixed on the blue shinning waters of the Lake that the west window showed,

🎧 24

양손으로 턱chin을 받치고propped, 서쪽 창으로 내다보이는 반짝이는 호수의 파란 물빛에 시선을 고정한fixed 채,

그녀는 머나먼 환상의 꿈나라에 있었다.

she was _____

_____.

* **gorgeous** 아주 멋진, 화려한
* **dreamland** 꿈나라, 유토피아

그녀는 머나먼 환상의 꿈나라를 돌아다니느라
아무것도 들리지도 보이지도 않았다.

she was far away in a gorgeous dreamland

_____ .

그녀는 머나먼 환상의 꿈나라를 돌아다니느라
자신만의 멋진 풍경 이외에는
아무것도 들리지도 보이지도 않았다.

she was far away in a gorgeous dreamland

hearing and seeing nothing other _____

_____ .

* vision 시야

그녀는 머나먼 환상의 꿈나라를 돌아다니느라
자신만의 멋진 풍경 이외에는 아무것도
들리지도 보이지도 않았다.

she was far away in a gorgeous dreamland
hearing and seeing nothing other than
her own wonderful visions.

길버트 블라이스는 익숙하지 않았다.

26

Gilbert Blythe wasn't _____.

길버트 블라이스는
실패하는 것에 **익숙하지 않았다.**

Gilbert Blythe wasn't used to

_____ .

* **failing** 실패, 실수

길버트 블라이스는

만드는 일이 실패하는 것에 익숙하지 않았다.

Gilbert Blythe wasn't used to
failing _____ .

길버트 블라이스는
여자아이가 자신을 쳐다보도록 만드는 일이
실패하는 것에 익숙하지 않았다.

Gilbert Blythe wasn't used to
failing to make

_____ .

길버트 블라이스는
여자아이가 자신을 쳐다보도록 만드는 일이
실패하는 것에 익숙하지 않았다.

Gilbert Blythe wasn't used to
failing to make
a girl look at him.

She should look at him, that red-haired Shirley girl with the little pointed chin and the big eyes that weren't like the eyes of any other girl in Avonlea school.

뽀족한 턱에, 에이번리의 다른 여학생들 같지 않게 눈이 유난히 큰 빨간 머리red-haired 셜리 소녀도 자신을 보아야 한다고 생각했다.

🎧 27

Gilbert reached across the aisle,
picked up the end of Anne's long red
braid, held it out at arm's length and
said in a piercing whisper:

"Carrots! Carrots!"

길버트가 통로 건너편으로 팔을 뻗어 길게 땋은 앤의 빨간 머리
끝을 들어올리고는 날카롭게piercing 속삭였다whisper.

"홍당무! 홍당무!"

그러자 앤이 쏘아보았다.

Then Anne _____ .

* **glared** 쏘아보았다(원 glare)

그러자 앤이 길버트를 쏘아보았다.

Then Anne glared _____.

그러자 앤이 잡아먹을 듯
길버트를 쏘아보았다.

Then Anne glared at Gilbert

_____ .

* as if 마치 ~하려는 듯이

그러자 앤이 잡아먹을 듯
길버트를 쏘아보았다.

Then Anne glared at Gilbert
as if she were going to eat him.

She did more than look.

"You hateful boy!"

She exclaimed loudly. Bam!

앤은 쏘아보는 것만으로 그치지 않았다.

"이 비열한hateful 놈아!"

앤이 흥분해서passionately 소리쳤다exclaimed.

퍽thwack!

Anne had put the slate down on
Gilbert's head and broke it. Avonlea
school always enjoyed a scene.
And this was an especially enjoyable one.

앤이 석판slate을 길버트의 머리에 내리쳐서 두 동강을 내버렸다.
에이번리 학교 아이들은 항상 소동scene을 좋아했다.
그리고 이번 일은 특히especially 재미있는enjoyable 사건이었다.

Everybody said "oh" in horrified delight.

"Anne Shirley, what does this mean?"

Mr. Phillips said angrily.

Anne gave no answer.

모두 '오!' 하며 두려우면서도in horrified 기쁨delight에 찬 탄성을 내질렀다.

"앤 셜리, 이게 뭐하는 짓이냐?"

필립스 선생님이 화난angrily 목소리로 말했다.

앤은 아무 대답도 하지 않았다.

이건 요구였다.

It was _____ .

* demand 요구

이건 살과 피의 요구였다.

It was a demand of _____ .

* flesh 살, 피부

이건 너무 큰 살과 피의 요구였다.

It was a demand of flesh and blood

_____ .

그녀에게 기대하기엔

너무 큰 살과 피의 요구였다.

It was a demand of flesh and blood too big

_____ .

그녀가 '홍당무'라고 불려진 것을 이야기하는 것은
그녀에게 기대하기엔
너무 큰 살과 피의 요구였다.

IIt was a demand of flesh and blood too big
to expect from her _____

_____.

그녀가 '홍당무'라고 불려진 것을 이야기하는 것은
그녀에게 기대하기엔
너무 큰 살과 피의 요구였다.

It was a demand of flesh and blood too big to expect from her to talk that she was called "carrots."

Gilbert spoke up stoutly.

"It was my fault Mr. Phillips. I teased her."

길버트가 용감하게|stoutly 입을 열었다.

"제 잘못입니다, 필립스 선생님. 제가 앤을 놀렸어요.teased."

But Mr. Phillips paid no heed to Gilbert.

"Anne, go and stand on the platform in front of the blackboard for the rest of the afternoon."

필립스 선생님은 길버트의 말에 아랑곳하지heed 않았다.

"앤, 남은 오후 시간 동안 칠판blackboard 앞 교단platform 위에 서 있어라."

"이런 학생을 보다니 **안타까운 일이구나.**"

"I am so sorry _____."

* pupil 학생, 제자

"내 학생 중에 이런 아이가 있다니
  안타까운 일이구나."

"I am so sorry to see a pupil _____."

"내 학생 중에 이렇게 못된 아이가 있다니

 안타까운 일이구나."

"I am so sorry to see a pupil of mine

_____.**"**

* wicked 못된, 고약한

"내 학생 중에 이렇게 못된 아이가 있다니
　안타까운 일이구나."

"I am so sorry to see a pupil of mine with such a wicked soul."

Mr. Phillips took a piece of chalk and wrote on the blackboard above her head.

필립스 선생님이 앤의 머리 위_{above her head} **칠판에 분필**_{chalk} **로 이렇게 썼다.**

"Ann Shirley has a very bad temper.
Anne Shirley must learn to control
her temper."

"앤 셜리는 성질temper이 고약합니다.
앤 셜리는 화를 참는 법을 배워야 합니다."

필립스 선생님은 그것을 읽었다.

🎧 35

Mr. Phillips _____.

필립스 선생님은 큰 소리로 읽었다.

Mr. Phillips read it out _____ .

필립스 선생님은

1학년 아이들까지 알아들을 수 있게

큰 소리로 읽었다.

Mr. Phillips read it out loud

_____

_____ .

* so that ~하도록 하다

필립스 선생님은 아직 글을 읽을 줄 모르는 1학년 아이들까지 알아들을 수 있게 큰 소리로 읽었다.

Mr. Phillips read it out loud

so that even the first-year children _____

_____ could understand.

필립스 선생님은 글을 읽을 줄 모르는 1학년 아이들까지 알아들을 수 있게 큰 소리로 읽었다.

Mr. Phillips read it out loud
so that even the first-year children
who still couldn't read could understand.

When the class was dismissed,

Anne went out with her red head held high.

Gilbert Blythe tried to intercept her at the

door.

수업이 끝나자 When the class was dismissed 앤은 빨간 머리를 빳빳이

들고 밖으로 나왔다.

길버트 블라이스가 현관문에서 앤을 막아서려 intercept 했다.

"I'm awfully sorry. I made fun of your hair, Anne," he whispered.
Anne passed him coldly, without any sign of hearing.

"네 머리를 갖고 놀려서 정말awfully 미안해."
길버트가 속삭였다.
앤은 들은 척도 하지 않고 차갑게 휙 지나가 버렸다.

어느 날 앤은 배에 올랐다.

One day, Anne _____.

어느 날 앤은 혼자 배에 올랐다.

One day, Anne got on a boat _____.

어느 날 앤은 친구들 앞에서
혼자 배에 올랐다.

One day, Anne got on a boat alone

_____ .

* in front of ~앞에서

어느 날 앤은
'백합 아가씨의 죽음'을 흉내 내려고
친구들 앞에서 혼자 배에 올랐다.

**One day, Anne got on a boat alone
in front of her friends**

_____

_____ .

* imitate 흉내내다
* The death of the Lily Maid' '백합 아가씨의 죽음'

어느 날 앤은 시의 한 장면인
'백합 아가씨의 죽음'을 흉내 내려고
친구들 앞에서 혼자 배에 올랐다.

One day, Anne got on a boat alone
in front of her friends
to imitate 'the death of the Lily maid',

_____ .

* poem 시

어느 날 앤은 시의 한 장면인
'백합 아가씨의 죽음'을 흉내 내려고
친구들 앞에서 혼자 배에 올랐다.

One day, Anne got on a boat alone
in front of her friends
to imitate 'the death of the Lily maid',
a scene of a poem.

얼마 동안, 앤은 즐겼다.

For a few minutes,

_____.

얼마 동안 앤은
이 낭만적인 상황을 즐겼다.

For a few minutes,

Anne enjoyed _____.

얼마 동안 앤은

이 낭만적인 상황을 마음껏 즐겼다.

For a few minutes,

Anne enjoyed this romantic situation

_____ .

* heart's content 흡족하게, 실컷

얼마 동안 앤은 천천히 떠내려가며,
이 낭만적인 상황을 마음껏 즐겼다.

For a few minutes,

Anne enjoyed this romantic situation

to her heart's content, _____.

* drift 떠가다, 표류하다

얼마 동안 앤은 천천히 떠내려가며,
이 낭만적인 상황을 마음껏 즐겼다.

For a few minutes,
Anne enjoyed this romantic situation
to her heart's content, drifting slowly.

Then something not romantic at all
happened. The boat began to leak. It was
because of the sharp stake at the landing.

다음 순간 전혀 낭만적이지 않은 상황이 벌어졌다.
배에 물이 새기leak 시작한 것이다. 출발 지점the landing의 뾰족한
sharp 말뚝stake 때문이었다.

In a few moments, Anne stood up
and picked up her golden cloth.
She looked blankly at a big crack in
the bottom of her boat. The water was
literally pouring.

🎧 39

이내 앤은 황금 옷을 들고 일어나 보트 바닥의
커다란 틈새crack로 문자 그대로 콸콸 쏟아져pouring 들어오는
물을 멍하니blankly 바라봐야만 했다.

그것은 오래 걸리지 않았다.

It did not _____.

깨닫는 데는 **오래 걸리지 않았다.**

It did not take long _____ .

그녀가 자신이 위험에 빠졌다는 걸 깨닫는 데는
오래 걸리지 않았다.

It did not take long to realize

_____ .

그녀가 자신이 위험에 빠졌다는 걸 깨닫는 데는
오래 걸리지 않았다.

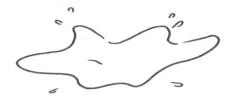

It did not take long to realize

that she was in a danger.

The boat drifted under the bridge and then sank in midstream. Ruby, Jane, and Diana, already awaiting it on the lower headland, saw it disappear before their very eyes.

다리 밑을 떠내려가던 배는 도중에midstream 가라앉아버렸다sank. 이미 아래쪽 갑판에서 기다리고 있던awaiting 루비, 제인, 다이애나는 자신들의 눈앞에서before their very eyes 배가 사라지는disappear 모습을 똑똑히 보았고,

They had not a doubt that Anne had gone down with it. For a moment they stood still, white as sheets, frozen with horror at the tragedy.

🎧 41

그들은 배와 함께 앤도 틀림없이|not a doubt 가라앉았다고 생각했다. 그 비극적인tragedy 장면을 보며 아이들은 한동안 백지장처럼 하얘진 얼굴로 공포horror에 질려 꿈쩍도 못하고frozen 서 있었다.

Then, screaming at the tops of their voices,
they started to run up through the woods,
never pausing as they crossed the main road
to glance the way of the bridge.

그러다가 갑자기 찢어질 듯한 비명을 내지르며 미친 듯이 숲으로 달려 올라갔고, 한 번도 멈추지 않고never pausing 다리 쪽은 볼 생각도 않은 채 큰길로 지나갔다.

Anne heard them shouting,
desperately clinging to her
precarious foothold. Help would
come soon, but meanwhile her posture was
very uncomfortable.

🎧 42

앤은 친구들의 비명 소리를 들으며, 불안한 발판precarious foothold
위에 필사적으로desperately 매달려 있었다clinging.
이제 곧 구원의 손길이 닿을 터였지만 그때까지 자세posture가 너
무도 불편했다uncomfortable.

이윽고 그 순간, 그녀는 생각했다.

Then, at the very moment

_____ .

이윽고 그 순간,
그녀는 버티지 못하겠다고 생각했다.

Then, at the very moment she thought

_____ .

이윽고 그녀는
팔과 손목이 아파 정말 더 이상은
버티지 못하겠다고 생각했다.

Then, at the very moment she thought
she could no longer bear the pain, _____

_____ ,

* ache 아프다, 쑤시다; 아픔
* wrists 손목들, 관절들

이윽고 팔과 손목이 아파
버티지 못하겠다고 생각한 그 순간,
길버트 블라이스가 왔다.

Then, at the very moment she thought
she could no longer bear the pain of her arms
and wrists, _____.

이윽고 팔과 손목이 아파

버티지 못하겠다고 생각한 그 순간,

길버트 블라이스가

하면 앤드루스 씨의 낚싯배를 타고 노를 저어 왔다!

Then, at the very moment she thought
she could no longer bear the pain of her arms
and wrists, Gilbert Blythe came

_____

_____!

* rowing 노를 저으며(원 row)
* Harman Andrews 하먼 앤드루스

이윽고 팔과 손목이 아파
버티지 못하겠다고 생각한 그 순간,
길버트 블라이스가
하먼 앤드루스 씨의 낚싯배를 타고 노를 저어 왔다!

Then, at the very moment she thought
she could no longer bear the pain of her arms
and wrists, Gilbert Blythe came
rowing in a Harmon Andrews's fishing boat!

Gilbert reluctantly rowed toward at her,
but Anne jumped on the shore refusing his
help. "I'm much obliged to you." she said
arrogantly as she turned away.

길버트가 주저하며reluctantly 앤에게 노를 저어 갔으나,

앤은 그의 도움을 거부하고 물가로 뛰어올랐다jumped on.

"너에게 큰 신세를 졌어obliged."

앤은 돌아서며 거만하게arrogantly 말했다.

But Gilbert had also sprung from the

boat and grabbed her arm.

"Anne," he said hurriedly,

"Look here. Can't we be good friends?"

그러나 길버트 역시 배에서 내리더니 앤의 팔을 잡았다grabbed.

"앤." 그는 다급하게hurriedly 말했다.

"나 좀 봐. 우리 좋은 친구로 지내면 안 될까?"

"정말 미안해."

"I'm _____ sorry."

"네 머리에 대해 놀린 건 **정말 미안해.**"

"I'm awfully sorry _____

_____**."**

"저번에 네 머리에 대해 놀린 건
정말 미안해."

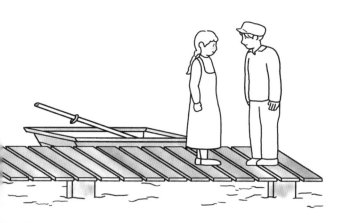

"I'm awfully sorry I made fun of your hair _____."

"저번에 네 머리에 대해 놀린 건
정말 미안해."

"I'm awfully sorry I made fun of your hair
that time."

"I didn't mean to put you to shame. I only meant it for a joke. Besides, it's so long ago.

"장난으로 그랬던 거지, 널 부끄럽게 만들_{put to shame} 생각은 없었어. 게다가_{besides} 그건 오래전 일이잖아.

I think your hair is really pretty now.

Honestly I do. Let's be friends."

지금은 네 머리가 아주 예쁘다고 생각해. 정말이야.

우리 친구로 지내자."

"No," she said coldly, "I shall never be friends with you, Gilbert Blythe.
And I don't want to be!"

"싫어." 앤은 차갑게coldly 말했다.
"난 너랑 친구가 될 수 없어, 길버트 블라이스.
그러고 싶지 않다고!"

🎧 47

"All right!" Gilbert jumped into his boat with an angry color in his cheeks.

"I'll never ask you to be friends again, Anne Shirley. And I don't care either!"

"그래!"

길버트가 화가 나서 벌겋게 달아오른 얼굴_{angry color in his cheeks}로 배에 올라탔다.

"다시는 너랑 친구하자고 안 하겠어, 앤 셜리. 나도 너 신경 안 써!"

앤은 슬픈 소식을 접했다.

Anne _____ **the sad news.**

앤은 하늘이 무너지는 것과 같은
슬픈 소식을 접했다.

Anne heard the sad news

_____.

* **struck** 충격을 줬다

앤은 충격과 함께 하늘이 무너지는 것과 같은
슬픈 소식을 접했다.

Anne heard the sad news

which struck her _____.

앤은 바쁘던 어느 날 충격과 함께
하늘이 무너지는 것과 같은
슬픈 소식을 접했다.

Anne heard the sad news

which struck her with a shock

_____.

앤은 준비로 바쁘던 어느 날
충격과 함께 하늘이 무너지는 것과 같은
슬픈 소식을 접했다.

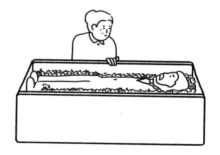

Anne heard the sad news
which struck her with a shock
while being busy _____.

* preparation 준비

앤은 대학에 진학하기 위한 준비로
바쁘던 어느 날 충격과 함께
하늘이 무너지는 것과 같은
슬픈 소식을 접했다.

Anne heard the sad news
which struck her with a shock
while being busy in preparation

_____.

앤은 대학에 진학하기 위한 준비로
바쁘던 어느 날 충격과 함께
하늘이 무너지는 것과 같은
슬픈 소식을 접했다.

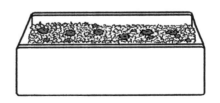

Anne heard the sad news
which struck her with a shock
while being busy in preparation
to go to a college.

Matthew died suddenly of heart attack right after hearing of the bankruptcy of the bank that he saved all the money in. Anne and Marilla consoled each other.

매슈 아저씨가 전 재산을 맡긴 은행의 파산bankruptcy 소식을 듣고 그 충격으로 심장마비를 일으켜 갑자기 돌아가신 것이다. 앤과 마릴라는 서로의 슬픔을 위로했다consoled .

🎧 49

Marilla couldn't live alone because her eyesight was failing. Because of that, Anne gave up going to a college deciding to stay with Marilla. When Ann visited a neighbor, aunt Mrs. Lynde, She said,

---

시력_{eyesight}이 나빠지고 있는 마릴라는 혼자서 지낼 수 없게 되었다. 이 때문에 앤은 마릴라와 함께 지내기 위해 대학 진학을 포기했다. 앤이 옆집의 린드 아주머니를 방문했을 때, 아주머니가 말했다.

"앤, 난 들었다."

"Anne, I _____."

"앤, 난 네가 포기했다고 들었다."

"Anne, I heard _____."

"앤, 난 네가 생각을 접었다고 들었다."

"Anne, I heard you've given up
_____."

* notion 생각, 관념

"앤, 난 네가 대학에 가겠다는
생각을 접었다고 들었다."

"Anne, I heard you've given up your notion
_____."

"앤, 난 네가 대학에 가겠다는
생각을 접었다고 들었다."

"Anne, I heard you've given up your notion of going to college."

"정말 기뻤다."

"I was _____."

"그걸 들으니 정말 기뻤다."

"I was really glad _____."

"그걸 들으니 정말 기뻤다."

"I was really glad to hear it."

"넌 교육을 받았어."

"You_____."

"넌 충분한 교육을 받았어."

"You have been educated _____."

"넌 여자로서는 충분한 교육을 받았어."

"You have been educated enough

_____."

"넌 여자로서는 충분한 교육을 받았어."

"You have been educated enough as a woman."

"I don't believe in girls going to college with men to fill their heads with Latin, Greek and all that nonsense."

"난 여자애들이 남자들과 같이 대학에 가서 라틴어Latin니 그리스어Greek니 쓸데없는 것nonsense들을 머릿속에 집어넣는fill 건 옳지 않다고 생각해."

"But I'm going to study Latin and
Greek just the same, Mrs. Lynde,"
said Anne laughing.

"하지만 저도 라틴어와 그리스어를
공부할 건데요, 린드 아주머니."
앤이 웃으면서 대꾸했다.

"전 인문 과정을 익힐 작정이에요."

"I'm _____ take my Arts course."

"**전 바로** 이곳에서

　인문 과정을 익힐 작정이에요."

"I'm going to take my Arts course
_____."

"전 바로 이곳에서

　인문 과정을 익히고 모두 공부할 작정이에요."

"I'm going to take my Arts course right here, _____."

"전 바로 이곳에서

　대학에서 배우는 **인문 과정을 익히고**

　모두 공부할 작정이에요."

"I'm going to take my Arts course right here, and study everything _____."

"전 바로 이곳에서
대학에서 배우는 인문 과정을 익히고
모두 공부할 작정이에요."

"I'm going to take my Arts course right here, and study everything that I would learn at college."

"I'm going to teach over at Carmody, you know."
"I don't know it. I guess you're going to teach right here in Avonlea, The trustees have decided to give you the school."

"아시겠지만, 전 카모디Carmody; 에이번리 주변 지명에서 교편을 잡을 거예요."
"그건 모르지. 내 생각엔 이곳 에이번리에서 가르치지 않을까 싶은데. 이사회trustees에서 너에게 학교자리를 주겠다고 결정했다던걸."

🎧 55

"Mrs. Lynde!" cried Anne, springing
to her feet in her surprise.

"I thought they had promised it to
Gilbert Blythe!"

"At first, they did."

"린드 아주머니!

앤이 놀라 벌떡 일어서며 소리쳤다.

"길버트 블라이스가 가르치기로 되어 있었잖아요!"

"처음엔 그랬었지."

"**그런데 길버트가 듣자마자**"

🎧 56

"But _____**,"**

"그런데 네가 지원했다는 소리를
길버트가 듣자마자"

"But as soon as Gilbert heard

_____,"

* applied 신청했다(원 apply)

"그런데 네가 그곳에 지원했다는 소리를
길버트가 듣자마자"

"But as soon as Gilbert heard
that you had applied _____,"

"그런데 네가 그곳에
지원했다는 소리를
듣자마자 길버트가 그들에게 찾아갔다지 뭐냐."

"But as soon as Gilbert heard
that you had applied for it,
_____."

* it 여기에서는 에이번리 학교를 가리킨다

"그런데 네가 에이번리 학교에
지원했다는 소리를 듣자마자
길버트가 그들에게 찾아갔다지 뭐냐."

"But as soon as Gilbert heard
that you had applied for it,
he went to them."

"그 애가 그들에게 말했단다."

"He _____."

"그 애가 자신은 지원을 취소한다고
그들에게 말했단다."

"He told them

_____.**"**

"그 애가

자신은 지원을 취소한다고 그들에게 말하고

제안했단다."

"He told them

he had withdrawn the application,

_____."

* offer 건의했다, 제안했다(원 suggest)

"그 애가

　자신은 지원을 취소한다고 그들에게 말하고

　대신 네 지원서를 통과시킬 것을 제안했단다."

"He told them

he had withdrawn the his application,

and offered _____."

* accept (신청, 임명 등을) 받아들이다, 수락하다

"그 애가
  자신은 지원을 취소한다고 그들에게 말하고
  대신 네 지원서를 통과시킬 것을 제안했단다."

"He told them

he had withdrawn the his application,

and offered to accept yours instead."

"He said he was going to teach at White Sands, and he will have his board to pay him at White Sands. Everybody knows he has to find his own way through college."

"자기는 화이트 샌즈White Sands; 에이번리 주변 지명에서 가르칠 거고, 자기를 지원해줄 이사회도 거기 있다고 말이야. 알다시피 대학도 자기 힘으로 가야 하는데."

🎧 58

"I don't feel that I should accept it,"

murmured Anne.

"I mean... I don't think I ought to let

Gilbert make such a sacrifice for... for me."

"그러면 안 될 것 같아요."

앤이 중얼거렸다murmured.

"그러니까… 길버트가 저 때문에…

그런 희생sacrifice 을 하게 할 수 없어요."

언덕 중간쯤 내려오자 키가 큰 청년이 나왔다.

59

Halfway down the hill,

_____.

언덕 중간쯤 내려오자 키가 큰 청년이
블라이스 씨 집 문에서 **나왔다.**

Halfway down the hill, a tall boy came out

_____ .

언덕 중간쯤 내려오자
키가 큰 청년이 휘파람을 불며
블라이스 씨 집 문에서 나왔다.

Halfway down the hill, a tall boy came

_____ out of the door of Mr. Blythe's

house.

언덕 중간쯤 내려오자
키가 큰 청년이 휘파람을 불며
블라이스 씨 집 문에서 나왔다.

Halfway down the hill, a tall boy came whistling out of the door of Mr. Blythe's house.

휘파람이 멈췄다.

The whistle _____.

휘파람이 그의 입술에서 **멈췄다.**

The whistle died _____.

앤을 알아보고는
휘파람이 그의 입술에서 멈췄다.

The whistle died on his lips

_____ .

앤을 알아보고는
휘파람이 그의 입술에서 멈췄다.

The whistle died on his lips
as he recognized Anne.

그는 공손하게 **모자를 벗었지만,**

Though he lifted his cap _____ **,**

* **lifted** 들어올렸다(원 lift)
* **courteously** 예의 바르게

그는 공손하게 모자를 벗었지만,

그는 지나쳤을 터였다.

Though he lifted his cap courteously,

_____.

* pass by 지나치다

그는 공손하게 모자를 벗었지만,
그는 조용히 지나쳤을 터였다.

Though he lifted his cap courteously,
he would have just passed by _____ .

그는 공손하게 모자를 벗었지만,
앤이 멈춰 서지 않았더라면
그는 조용히 지나쳤을 터였다.

Though he lifted his cap courteously,
he would have just passed by in silence,

_____.

그는 공손하게 모자를 벗었지만,
앤이 멈춰 서서
손을 내밀지 않았더라면
그는 조용히 지나쳤을 터였다.

Though he lifted his cap courteously,
he would have just passed by in silence,
if Anne had not stopped

_____ .

* **held out** (손 따위를) 내밀었다(원 hold out)

그는 공손하게 모자를 벗었지만,
앤이 멈춰 서서
손을 내밀지 않았더라면
그는 조용히 지나쳤을 터였다.

Though he lifted his cap courteously,
he would have just passed by in silence,
if Anne had not stopped
and held her hand out.

"난 고마워하고 싶어."

"I want _____."

"학교를 양보해줘서 **고마워**."

"I want to thank you

_____.**"**

"날 위해 **학교를 양보해줘서** 고마워."

"I want to thank you
for giving up the school _____."

"날 위해 학교를 양보해줘서 고마워."

"I want to thank you
for giving up the school for me."

"난 널 원해."

"I _____ you."

"난 네가 알아줬으면 좋겠어."

"I want you _____."

"내가 고마워하는 걸 알아줬으면 좋겠어."

"I want you to know _____."

* appreciate 고맙게 생각하다

"내가 고마워하는 걸 알아줬으면 좋겠어."

"I want you to know that I appreciate it."

"난 기뻤어."

"I was _____."

* **pleased** 즐겁게 했다, 즐거워진 (원 please)

"네게 도움이라도 줘서 **기뻤어.**"

"I was pleased

_____."

"네게 작은 도움이라도 줘서 기뻤어."

"I was pleased to give you

_____ help."

"네게 작은 도움이라도 줄 수 있어서 기뻤어."

"I was pleased to _____
give you even a little help."

"네게 작은 도움이라도 줄 수 있어서 기뻤어."

"I was pleased to be able to give you even a little help."

"Are we going to be friends after this?

Have you really forgiven my old fault?"

"그럼 우리 이제 친구가 되는 거니?

 내 옛날 실수를 정말 용서한forgiven 거야?"

Anne laughed and tried
unsuccessfully to pull her hand out.

앤이 웃으며 손을 빼려고 했지만 소용이 없었다unsuccessfully.

"난 널 용서했어."

"I _____ you."

* **forgave** 용서했다(원 forgive)

"난 그날 널 용서했어."

"I forgave you _____."

"난 그날 강가에서 널 용서했어."

"I forgave you that day _____."

"난 그날 강가에서 널 용서했어.

　나도 그땐 몰랐지만 말이야."

"I forgave you that day by the river
_____."

* although ~일지라도

"난 그날 강가에서 널 용서했어.
  나도 그땐 몰랐지만 말이야."

"I forgave you that day by the river although I didn't know it."

"We are going to be the best of friends," said Gilbert, with joy.

"우리는 최고의 친구가 될 거야."
길버트가 기뻐하며 말했다.

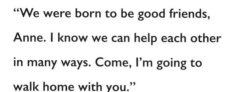

"We were born to be good friends, Anne. I know we can help each other in many ways. Come, I'm going to walk home with you."

"처음부터 우린 좋은 친구가 될 운명이었어, 앤. 서로 여러모로 도움이 될 거야. 가자, 집까지 바래다줄게."

마릴라가 앤을 궁금한 듯이 쳐다보았다.

Marilla looked _____ at Anne.

* **curiously** 신기한 듯이, 궁금한 듯이

앤이 부엌으로 들어오자
마릴라가 궁금한 듯이 쳐다보았다.

Marilla looked curiously at Anne

_____ .

앤이 부엌으로 들어오자
마릴라가 궁금한 듯이 쳐다보았다.

Marilla looked curiously at Anne
when she entered the kitchen.

"너와 길버트 블라이스가
  친한 사이인 줄은 몰랐구나."

n 69

"I didn't think _____

_____

_____."

"너와 길버트 블라이스가 서 있을 정도로
친한 사이인 줄은 몰랐구나."

"I didn't think you and Gilbert Blythe were such good friends _____."

"너와 길버트 블라이스가 문간에서 30분 동안이나 서 있을 정도로 친한 사이인 줄은 몰랐구나."

"I didn't think you and Gilbert Blythe were such good friends that you'd stand _____."

* half an hour 30분

"너와 길버트 블라이스가 문간에서 30분 동안이나

서서 얘기를 나눌 정도로

친한 사이인 줄은 몰랐구나."

"I didn't think you and Gilbert Blythe were such good friends that you'd stand for half an hour at the gate _____ ."

"너와 길버트 블라이스가 문간에서 30분 동안이나
서서 얘기를 나눌 정도로
친한 사이인 줄은 몰랐구나."

"I didn't think you and Gilbert Blythe were such good friends that you'd stand for half an hour at the gate talking to him."

"우리는 선의의 경쟁자였죠."

"We_____ good enemies."

* enemy 적, 경쟁상대

"우리는 선의의 경쟁자였죠."

"We've been good enemies."

"하지만 우리는 알게 됐어요.

71

"But we _____."

* found 알게 됐다(원 find)

"하지만 이게 훨씬 도움이 된다는 걸
 알게 됐어요."

"But we found _____

_____**."**

* sensible 똑똑한, 현명한

"하지만 좋은 친구로 지내는 게

　휠씬 도움이 된다는 걸 알게 됐어요."

"But we found that it will be much more sensible _____."

"하지만 앞으로는

좋은 친구로 지내는 게 훨씬 도움이 된다는 걸

알게 됐어요."

"But we found that it will be
much more sensible to be good friends
_____."

"하지만 앞으로는
 좋은 친구로 지내는 게 훨씬 된다는 걸
 알게 됐어요."

"But we found that it will be
much more sensible to be good friends
in the future."

"Were we really there half an hour?

"우리가 정말 30분 동안이나 거기 있었어요?

It seemed just a few minutes."

72

몇 분밖에 안 된 것 같았는데seemed."

"하지만 정말 많은 것들이 있거든요."

"But, there are _____**."**

"하지만 우리가 이야기하지 못한 것들이
  많거든요."

"But, there are so many things
_____."

"하지만 우리가 지난 5년 동안 이야기하지 못한
것들이 많거든요, 마릴라 아주머니."

"But, there are so many things
we haven't talked about _____,
Marilla."

"하지만 우리가 지난 5년 동안 이야기하지 못한
것들이 많거든요, 마릴라 아주머니."

"But there are so many things
we haven't talked about in five years,
Marilla."

앤의 꿈들은 작아졌다.

Anne's dreams _____.

그날 밤 이후로
앤의 꿈들은 작아졌다.

Anne's dreams have been small

_____.

집으로 돌아온 날 밤 이후로
앤의 꿈들은 작아졌다.

Anne's dreams have been small
since the night _____.

집으로 돌아와

그 자리에 앉아 있던 **밤 이후로**

앤의 꿈들은 작아졌다.

Anne's dreams have been small
since the night she returned home
_____ .

집으로 돌아와
그 자리에 앉아 있던 밤 이후로
앤의 꿈들은 작아졌다.

Anne's dreams have been small
since the night she returned home
and sat there.

하지만 앤은 알고 있었다,

만약 길이 좁다 해도,

🎧 75

But she knew

_____.

* path 작은 길, 오솔길
* narrow 폭이 좁은

하지만 앤은 알고 있었다,
만약 자신 앞에 놓인 길이 좁다 해도,

But she knew

that even if the path

was narrow,

하지만 앤은 알고 있었다,

만약 자신 앞에 놓인 길이 좁다 해도,

꽃이 피어나리라는 것을.

But she knew

that even if the path set before her

was narrow, _____ .

* bloom 꽃이 피다

하지만 앤은 알고 있었다,
만약 자신 앞에 놓인 길이 좁다 해도,
잔잔한 행복의 꽃이
피어나리라는 것을.

But she knew

that even if the path set before her

was narrow, flowers _____

would bloom.

* calm 잔잔한

하지만 앤은 알고 있었다,
만약 자신 앞에 놓인 길이 좁다 해도,
그 길을 따라 잔잔한 행복의 꽃이 피어나리라는 것을.

But she knew
that even if the path set before her
was narrow, flowers of calm happiness would
bloom _____.

하지만 앤은 알고 있었다,
만약 자신 앞에 놓인 길이 좁다 해도,
그 길을 따라 잔잔한 행복의 꽃이 피어나리라는 것을.

But she knew
that even if the path set before her
was narrow, flowers of calm happiness would
bloom along it.

Matthew and Marilla were brother and sister farming in Avonlea in Edward Island in Canada. They wanted to adopt a boy to help them to farm because neither of them had married even though they were middle age. Matthew and Marilla were waiting for the boy after they had applied for adoption. On the day the boy was supposed to come, Matthew went to the station to meet him. But, it was a skinny girl with red hair and freckles in her face that the orphanage sent them.

"Matthew, who's she? Where is the boy?"

"There wasn't any boy," said Matthew.

"There was only HER."

He nodded at the child remembering that he had never even asked her name.

"No boy! But we sent word to the orphanage to bring a boy."

"I couldn't leave her at the station alone no matter where the mistake had come in."

During this dialogue, the child was silent looking from one to the other.

Suddenly, she dropped her precious bag and sprang forward a step clasping her hands and yelled out.

"You don't want me because I'm not a boy! Nobody ever wanted me. I forgot that nobody had ever wanted me."

Matthew persuaded Marilla.

"Well, she's a real nice little thing, Marilla. It's kind of a pity to send her back when she wants to stay here so much. Think about it. She could be your good friend to talk to."

Matthew thought of Anne who was happy calling the ordinary path lined with apple trees a white road of joy, on his way home. Matthew kind of liked the talkative little girl. Marilla decided not to send her back. And that is how Anne began to live in the house with the green gables. Matthew and Marilla lived happily because of talkative Anne who was a child of imagination. Anne started a joyful journey with her best friend, Diana at school.

One September morning, Anne and Diana, two of the happiest little girls in Avonlea, were walking on the street to the school blithely.

"I guess Gilbert Blythe will be in school today," said Diana.

"He's been visiting his cousins. He's awfully handsome, Anne. And he teases the girls so much. He just torments them."

But, Diana's voice indicated that she rather liked having her life tormented than not.

"You'll have Gilbert in your class after this," said Diana,

"And he used to be the head of his class, I can tell you. You won't find it so easy to be first place after this, Anne."

When Mr. Phillips was in the back of the classroom hearing Latin from one of the students, Diana whispered to Anne.

"That's Gilbert Blythe sitting right across the aisle from you, Anne."

"Just look at him and see if you don't think he's handsome."

She had a good chance to do so because Gilbert Blythe was busy pinning the long yellow braid of a girl who sat in front of him to the back of her seat.

Presently Ruby Gillis stood up to give the math answer to the teacher; she fell back into her seat with a little shriek, believing that her hair was pulled out by the roots.

She began to cry and Gilbert had whisked the pin out of sight and was studying his history with the soberest face in the world. But after this, he looked at Anne and winked.

After school, Anne confided to Diana "I think your Gilbert Blythe is handsome. But I think he's very bold. Moreover, it isn't good manners to wink at a strange girl."

Gilbert Blythe was trying to make Anne Shirley look at him and failing utterly, because Anne was at that moment totally oblivious not only to the very existence of Gilbert Blythe, but of every other student in Avonlea school itself.

With her chin propped on her hands and her eyes fixed on the blue shinning waters of the Lake that the west window showed, she was far away in a gorgeous dreamland hearing and seeing nothing other than her own wonderful visions.

Gilbert Blythe wasn't used to failing to make a girl look at him. She should look at him, that red-haired Shirley girl with the little pointed chin and the big eyes that weren't like the eyes of any other girl in Avonlea school.

Gilbert reached across the aisle, picked up the end of Anne's long red braid, held it out at arm's length and said in a piercing whisper:

"Carrots! Carrots!"

Then Anne glared at Gilbert as if she were going to eat him.

She did more than look. "You hateful boy!" she exclaimed loudly. Bam! Anne had put the slate down on Gilbert's head and broke it.

Avonlea school always enjoyed a scene. And this was an especially enjoyable one.

Everybody said "oh" in horrified delight.

"Anne Shirley, what does this mean?" Mr. Phillips said angrily. Anne gave no answer. It was a demand of flesh and blood too big to expect from her to talk that she was called "carrots."

Gilbert spoke up stoutly. "It was my fault Mr. Phillips. I teased her."

But Mr. Phillips paid no heed to Gilbert.

"Anne, go and stand on the platform in front of the blackboard for the rest of the afternoon. I am so sorry to see a pupil of mine with such a wicked soul."

Mr. Phillips took a piece of chalk and wrote on the blackboard above her head.

"Anne Shirley has a very bad temper. Anne Shirley must learn to control her temper."

Mr. Phillips read it out loud so that even the first-year children who still couldn't read could understand.

When the class was dismissed, Anne went out with her red head held high. Gilbert Blythe tried to intercept her at the door.

"I'm awfully sorry I made fun of your hair, Anne," he whispered. But Anne passed him coldly, without any sign of hearing.

One day, Anne got on a boat alone in front of her friends to imitate 'the death of the Lily maid', a scene of a poem. For a few minutes, Anne enjoyed this romantic situation to her heart's content, drifting slowly.

Then something not romantic at all happened. The boat began to leak. It was because of the sharp stake at the landing. In a few moments, Anne stood up and picked up her golden cloth. She looked blankly at a big crack in the bottom of her boat. The water was literally pouring.

It did not take long to realize that she was in danger. The boat drifted under the bridge and then sank in midstream. Ruby, Jane, and Diana, already awaiting it on the lower headland, saw it disappear before their very eyes. They had not a doubt that Anne had gone down with it.

For a moment they stood still, white as sheets, frozen with horror at the tragedy. Then, screaming at the tops of their voices, they started to run up through the woods, never pausing as they crossed the main road to glance the way of the bridge.

Anne heard them shouting, desperately clinging to her precarious foothold. Help would come soon, but meanwhile her posture was very uncomfortable.

Then, at the very moment she thought she could no longer bear the pain of her arms and wrists, Gilbert Blythe came rowing in a Harmon Andrews's fishing boat!

Gilbert reluctantly rowed toward her, but Anne jumped on the shore refusing his help. "I'm much obliged to you." she said arrogantly as she turned away. But Gilbert had also sprung from the boat and grabbed her arm. "Anne," he said hurriedly, "Look here. Can't we be good friends? I'm awfully sorry I made fun of your hair that time. I didn't mean to put you to shame. I only meant it for a joke. Besides, it's so long ago. I think your hair is really pretty now. Honestly I do. Let's be friends."

"No," she said coldly, "I shall never be friends with you, Gilbert Blythe. And I don't want to be!"

"All right!" Gilbert jumped into his boat with an angry color in his cheeks. "I'll never ask you to be friends again, Anne Shirley. And I don't care either!"

Anne heard sad news which struck her with a shock while being busy in preparation to go to a college. Matthew died suddenly of a heart attack right after hearing of the bankruptcy of the bank that he saved all the money in. Anne and Marilla consoled each other.

Marilla couldn't live alone because her eyesight was failing. Because of that, Anne gave up going to a college deciding to stay with Marilla. When Anne visited a neighbor, aunt Mrs. Lynde, she said,

"Anne, I heard you've given up your notion of going to college. I was really glad to hear it. You have been educated enough as a woman.

I don't believe in girls going to college with men to fill their heads with Latin, Greek and all that nonsense."

"But I'm going to study Latin and Greek just the same, Mrs. Lynde," said Anne laughing.

"I'm going to take my Arts course right here, and study everything that I would learn at college. I'm going to teach over at Carmody, you know."

"I don't know it. I guess you're going to teach right here in Avonlea. The trustees have decided to give you the school."

"Mrs. Lynde!" cried Anne, springing to her feet in her surprise.

"I thought that they had promised it to Gilbert Blythe!"

"At first, they did. But as soon as Gilbert heard that you had applied for it, he went to them. He told them he had withdrawn the application, and offered to accept yours instead. He said he was going to teach at White Sands, and he will have his board to pay him at White Sands. Everybody knows he has to find his own way through college."

"I don't feel that I should accept it." murmured Anne.

"I mean... I don't think I ought to let Gilbert make such a sacrifice for... for me."

Halfway down the hill, a tall boy came whistling out of the door of Mr. Blythe's house. The whistle died on his lips as he recognized Anne.

Though he lifted his cap courteously, he would have just passed by in silence, if Anne had not stopped and held her hand out.

"I want to thank you for giving up the school for me. I want you to know that I appreciate it."

"I was pleased to be able to give you even a little help. Are we going to be friends after this? Have you really forgiven my old fault?"

Anne laughed and tried unsuccessfully to pull her hand out.

"I forgave you that day by the river, although I didn't know it."

"We are going to be the best of friends," said Gilbert with joy.

"We were born to be good friends, Anne. I know we can help each other in many ways. Come, I'm going to walk home with you."

Marilla looked curiously at Anne when she entered the kitchen.

"I didn't think you and Gilbert Blythe were such good friends that you'd stand for half an hour at the gate talking to him."

"We've been good enemies. But we found it will be much more sensible to be good friends in the future. Were we really there half an hour? It seemed just a few minutes. But there are so many things we haven't talked about in five years, Marilla."

Anne's dreams have been small since the night she returned home and sat there. But she knew that even if the path set before her was narrow, flowers of calm happiness would bloom along it.